Becoming Visible:
Emerging to Greater Heights Vol.1

By:
Nurse Candyce Pirtle-Smalls

Table of Contents

Part 1: See Me

Part 2: Hear Me

Part 3: Believe Me

Part 4: Witness Me

Books by the Author

Mindful Meal Prep: Clean, Delicious Recipes for Weight Loss

Becoming Visible: Emerging to Greater Heights Vol.1 Anthology

7 Courageous Women Spreading their Wings with the Courage to Fly Higher

Women of the World Anthology

(International Global Book)

Primary Author Elle Ballard, WOTWN Women of the World Network

Story: African American Culture, Health, Wellness, Generational Bondage and Overcoming it

"The Princess Warrior"

Acknowledgements

All thanks to my Heavenly Father God, the one and only Savior Jesus Christ for using me as a vessel to lead, evolve, empower, exchange and emerge with women all over the globe.

"For your glory"

God, if it makes me uncomfortable, even if I don't understand it, I just want to be where you are.

-Tasha Cobbs Leonard

I wish to thank the following people:

The board of the F.I.T. Butterfly Innovation Inc. Nonprofit Organization Walnut Creek, CA.

Thank you for believing in my vision and helping launch and birth F.I.T. (Female Inspired Transformation) Butterfly Innovation Inc. 2019. My loving and patient husband, Anthony Smalls, President of F.I.T. Butterfly, thank you for believing in me. I look forward to taking our stories and entrepreneurship into schools, career day, summer programs and sharing art therapy and expressive arts with the youth. Treasurer Joe Ann Hampton my dear mother, my best friend, my rock, thank you for keeping us on our toes and ensuring our organization runs smoothly.

Mr. Kelly Cole and team at Publishing Advantage Group in Bristol, Virginia for partnering with us for our 2x bestseller and making the Butterfly Project and Becoming Visible vision into reality for the Elite winning circle.

Our Ohana of OE, Office Evolution Walnut Creek, Ca Dawn Lopshire, Rhett and Callie for being one of the first to partner with F.I.T. Butterfly, for providing training rooms and services to facilitate wellness and training workshops.

Andrea Taylor, thank you for working in the capacity of the facilitator role along with co-coaching co-authors. We have spent many hours behind the scenes executing a clear vision and strategic path for this project.

Chaplain Jaqueline Quillens, my dear Mother in Law, thank you for your spiritual guidance and covering. Women are in healing as it is healing season. When we hosted our 1st Annual Woman 2 Woman Empowerment Brunch sponsored by F.I.T. Butterfly Innovation Inc. and the tears were flowing that day, God was all through the room as we discussed relationships (R.A.M.) rape, abuse, molestation, human trafficking, health and wellness, suicide, emotions and mental health. I was honored to be a guest speaker to a community of 50 women. The power of I am Woman "Superwoman" by Alicia Keys was at an all-time high.

Special thanks to all of our courageous co-authors, we could not have done this without you:

Teisha Levi LMFT, Tracey Frison, Ericka Parker, Shardae Jones, Tamela Gospel, Charlie on the Spot "Charleszetta Baldwin" Stylist, you ladies have found the courage to fly through the pandemic of COVID-19 and step into the uncertain future in order to take the steps to build your legacy. You ladies have put yourselves on the front line as an essential leader, not to be silenced, in order to save another soul. I love you. *We are stronger together!*

Most of all, thank you to Inner Healing F.I.T. Butterfly Community. You all are the reason our foundation is going. So many women, from all different walks of life, with different backgrounds and a similar story. We do this for you. Our safe space is a container to evolve, empower, exchange and emerge together. You are not alone.

Thank you to all the organizations behind the scenes who we have partnered with, such as: Extended Arms Bay Area, Family Justice Center, STAND for Families Free of Justice and Narika Bay Area.

Majestic Heart's Founder Kanisha Jackson, thank you for giving a space for women to share their trauma through storytelling. You have opened so many doors with just one interview, my very first interview, where I shared my story of being a survivor.

And lastly, thank you to Colleen & Deana at I Spotify podcast for my second interview of speaking my truth in Episode 15: Use Self-Love and Mindfulness to Break the Emotional Bonds of Domestic Violence.

Dedication

I dedicate this journey to all the young girls and women who were once lost in the storm, not seen, heard or believed. To the younger version of my mother. Thank you for not giving up on me. Thank you for being my rock and giving me everything you could and knew. You taught me how to survive and power through the darkest moments. Together we will break this generation of pain and push through our purpose for the upcoming generations of mothers, daughters, wives, sisters, aunts and nieces.

To the younger version of me, never give up on you, you never know who you will grow up to become. It gets better, I promise. You never know whose life you will save through your pain and shame. It's bigger than you baby girl. Your test will become your testimony, your mess, your message, and your wounds will be your beauty marks. I love you and remember your self-love will be your best love.

To those who do not know God or may know God but didn't allow him to carry you through the storm, I encourage you to surrender; his love is the best love and the journey is impossible to thrive without him.

Foreword
by Teisha Y. Levi, LMFT

What feelings come up for you when you think of past experiences? Are the feelings comforting like walking on soft sand or are they painful like the feeling of walking on rocks along the beach?

This compelling book highlights a series of stories that are designed to do just that—make you think about your own experiences! The individual stories should move you to a place of hope and empathy for the writer and compassion for yourself.

In a world filled with Boss Ladies, we must uplift each other during times of hardship and bliss. The following stories are from women, authors, professionals, and leaders who come from a variety of various backgrounds and experiences. Each writer brings the unique gift of her own experience. Their stories will resonate with you, the reader, as if it were your own. We have all experienced some form of trauma, hardship and maybe even abandonment. No matter the storm we can all flourish through prayer, self-love and the strength to reach prodigious outcomes.

As a Licensed Marriage and Family Therapist and active mental health provider, I work with several individuals who come to me with their stories seeking a solution for personal growth. My purpose of giving and impacting others' lives in the area of mental wellness has led me to discover that we all share a common core value: to live a rich and fulfilling life. Certainly, therapeutic services are available to support us in moving towards self-forgiveness and self-love, while giving us the skills for overall functional improvements. Therefore, it has been my purpose to listen, understand and guide individuals to a place of hope and empathy for themselves, their experiences, and for others.

So, I challenge you, the reader, to experience this two-fold body of work, designed to move you closer to your purpose in life, with personal stories, resources, and next stages. Seek and understand your purpose in life as you uphold hope and compassion for yourself.

Teisha Yvonne Levi, LMFT

Licensed Marriage and Family Therapist, #101104

Oakland, CA

teishalevi@gmail.com

www.mentalwellnesswithteisha.com

Foreword
by Chaplain Jacqueline Quillens

C andyce Pirtle-Smalls is a woman with many crowns and inscriptions, but her greatest accessory is her authentic love for others. Candyce must be commended on her ability to jointly fit this alliance of co-authors together for Becoming Visible: Emerging to Greater Heights Vol.1.

Many people want to change, but many are not willing to go through the long-lasting process change requires. The process to become a more powerful, brilliant, gorgeous, and better version of you will take work. This means taking a shift in how we see ourselves by casting off all negative labels and characteristics that life tosses our way. These women are self-reliant and have been gracefully transformed to unfold and distribute their life-changing healing wings to the world.

We hear a lot about transparency, and I believe the authors of Becoming Visible: Emerging to Greater Heights are as transparent as it gets. They leave no room for assumption or misunderstanding of what they have endured. It takes courage to confront what brings us physical or mental pain. The ability to say "I am forgiven of my past life of abuse, family dysfunction, attempted suicide, control, forced abortion, and rape" has set these women free! Self-forgiveness prevailed for these women to emerge and truly fly free.

Becoming Visible: Emerging to Greater Heights not only teaches women of every generation how to take control over their life, but it is also a self-help book that teaches how inside transformation must take place in order for outward transformation to emerge. I believe what compelled each of these women to be free from systemic pain is the option to know there was freedom on the other side of their hurt, pain, and shame.

Becoming Visible: Emerging to Greater Heights will encourage women to be refined through their pain and suffering, to achieve, and to emerge rejuvenated. This is their time and season to emerge as Esther's to bring restorative, healthy healing to women of every tribe, tongue, and generation.

Chaplain Jacqueline Quillens

Pittsburg, CA

mahogany504q@gmail.com

Introduction

W hat if your truth is bigger than you and it could set others FREE?

If this book reached your fingertips, it is not by accident. After writing my first book <u>Mindful Meal Prep: Clean, Delicious Recipes for Weight Loss</u> and making the bestseller list, I felt I needed to share my authentic pain behind emotional eating that caused me to weigh nearly 200 pounds. I viewed myself as a butterfly as there are four stages of the butterfly life cycle: the egg, the larvae (caterpillar), the pupa (chrysalis), and the adult butterfly.

I always considered myself a diamond in the rough, which leads me back to my 6th grade science project at North Hills, Christian School on the NorthSide of Vallejo, CA where I grew up. I developed a newfound obsession with butterflies and decided to research the Monarch Butterfly series. I soon thought that my life, relationships, marriage and career went through different cycles of stages. I was going through a transformation, or metamorphosis, as a butterfly does during its lifecycle.

Transformation: Dramatic change in form of appearance

The Caterpillar Stage: This stage represents the learning stage of growth, consuming as much growth and knowledge of myself.

To many it represents learning about business and mastering your craft through education, webinars, workshops and conferences. This is the stage of inspiration and excitement.

Let's rewind back to four years ago, when I was 4 pounds shy of weighing 200 pounds. I was comfortable with being uncomfortable. My marriage flame was dimmed due to me lacking confidence, and I dreaded looking into the mirror each day and night. Every night before bed I would look in my long room mirror and tug up and down on the mid area of my body, imagining how I'd look with a flatter stomach.

That was the powerful moment of a desperate need for change. I came to the realization that my cup was empty and that the only one who could fill it up with comfort, love and abundance was me, myself and I.

A written excerpt from <u>Mindful Meal Prep: Clean,</u> <u>Delicious Recipes for Weight Loss</u>

"The Salutary Princess Warrior"

As I look in the mirror, I see and appreciate how much I have transformed. Some people may wonder how I move so fast with limited time in the day. I tell them that we all get the same twenty-four hours; it's all about what you chose to spend your precious time on.

I simply stopped making excuses! Each day I one up myself. I compete against the old me. I want to be so much better than the old me. I'm indulged in my thoughts. I am free in my mind. I meditate, I pray, I speak my success and share my passion through my journey. I bring other women along with me on my journey—but only those who are willing to be 100% in.

I learned we can't change them, but we can change our damn self!

Look in the mirror! What do you see?

If you stare long enough, you'll dissect EVERYTHING. Every mark, every blemish, every crease. Instead of dissecting, open your mouth and start speaking your beauty, your power, your success and your affirmations into fruition.

Think it.

Say it.

Believe it!

But don't wait on it! Every day, I go out into the world, strap on my princess amour and I go BEAST mode!

Love, Pain, Passion

Salutary Princess Warrior

The Chrysalis Stage: This is the most intriguing stage of butterfly development, which appears catastrophic from the caterpillar. When the little crawler is fully grown, it can no longer eat, and it simply dangles from the branch.

The chrysalis stage of my transformation happened when I decided to invest in myself, attend boot camp, and eat clean.

From the outside, it may look like nothing is happening, however on the inside, MAJOR change is taking place as you are emerging into a butterfly.

The Power of Your Butterfly Effect: Beautiful Transformation and How it Will Grow Your Business and Life Full of Abundance

"Failure is an outcome that most of us dread but it has actually become a hot topic in business."

- Dr. Wyatt

The Butterfly Principle: *Transformation and Growth Through Failure*

It was a warm Spring in 2018, one year prior to writing my first book. I was invited to be a spotlight speaker for a networking group called Professional Women Regional Group. I showed up in a long-length black spaghetti-strap dress with a sheer, lime green collared button up, which I wore tied in a knot around my new 27-inch slim waistline. I chose to speak about the Butterfly Effect and how it will grow your business.

I stood in front of a table at Stanfords, a fancy restaurant in the heart of downtown Walnut Creek. A table that was filled with entrepreneurs and businesswomen, such as my business coach, graphic designers, and videographer. I shared the story of Oprah Winfrey's aha moments of stepping into her purpose and affirming her life with the role from her famous movie *The Color Purple*. It was a story from Oprah about how she became a believer. Her father always said he didn't want her to be an actress. But she spoke into existence the call that would change her life forever. The infamous call made by Steven Spielberg.

I presented my speech confidently, without looking at my notes. I was confident and didn't stutter on Steven Spielberg's name as I did during my practice runs at home in front of my husband. I was praised as I slayed the speech, with a lady from the audience saying that I was the new and upcoming Lisa Nichols. I was honored, as Lisa Nichols had been one of my mentors. I invested into one of her online programs to become a transformational speaker to the masses. I guess it was paying off, as my soul was burning with desire, dedication and determination.

Since then, I transformed my speech into a full course online program for my clients and organizations, and it has proven to be highly successful with the self-discovery stage of metamorphism.

I originally thought this would be a solo book, but God showed me visions. He made it clear that this was not a project to be done alone and that it was a Butterfly

Collection of stories about women who were ready to dive into the stages of metamorphosis and find the courage to break the silence, emerge and evolve together. To this day, a picture of a butterfly book is on my vision board.

Discovering Your Why Without Knowing Your Purpose

Our purpose fuels our passion in life. Without fueling our passion, we can't set our flame on fire. Oprah states that if we don't know our purpose, we are just existing in the universe. Just walking around...co-existing, breathing, hoping to be invisible, screaming internally. Not being heard.

Why do we do what we do?

October is National Domestic Violence Awareness Month

Did you know that the month of October is National Domestic Violence Awareness Month? Yes, it is! National Domestic Violence Awareness Month first began in 1981 by the National Coalition Against Domestic Violence as a Day of Unity to connect battered women advocates across the country.

Domestic violence affects millions, both women and men, of every race, religion, culture and status. It does not discriminate based on salary or ethnic background. And it's not just punches and black eyes—it's yelling, humiliation, stalking, manipulation, coercion, threats and isolation. It's stealing a paycheck, keeping tabs online, non-stop texting, constant use of the silent treatment, or calling someone stupid so often that they believe it.

In 1994, The Violence Against Women Act was passed. This landmark legislation, led by then Senator Joe Biden, combined new provisions that hold offenders accountable and provide programs and services for victims. Between 1993 and 2010, the overall rate of domestic violence dropped nearly two-thirds and state laws have reformed to address issues such as dating abuse in the workplace, stalking, employment discrimination and more.

Today, statistics show that 1 in 4 women have witnessed or been through a Domestic Violence (DV) relationship. This number is more frightening in the case of teens, with 1 in every 3 teens experiencing Teen Dating Violence.

Three and a half years ago, I weighed nearly 200 pounds of self-neglect and mindless eating. I ate to suppress my inner teenage trauma of a 3-year long physically and psychologically violent relationship. I internalized and hid the pain that domestic violence had caused.

It took many years, but I finally decided to look in the mirror and take control of my life. Today, I take my power back by eating well. I'm speaking up. I'm no longer a victim— but a survivor. I want to encourage you to do the same. Don't stay silent. It's time to speak up. Not just during the month of October, but all year around.

Join us on the transformational journey to inner-healing and taking our power back! Inner-Healing Workshop series is a safe space for teens and women of domestic violence, sexual assault, trauma, teenage pregnancy or codependency to be heard, seen, witnessed and believed so that they can experience recovery and healing.

This is a Survivor's Guide, built and designed to help women and adolescents thrive through their own storms of life. In this Survivor's Guide, you will learn seven Butterfly Principles that will help you to overcome trauma and make your shift into transformation.

As you turn the pages in this book, you will experience

seven extraordinary short stories where you will feel the writers' once pain and experience their once shame during dark and vulnerable portions of their lives.

These courageous women made a choice to write and shine a bright light as they light the torch and lead the way during the COVID-19 "storm" and "chaos." This will also be remembered as COVID-19 stay at home shelter in place or the Coronavirus disease pandemic storm.

> **Storm /stôrm/:** a violent disturbance of the atmosphere with strong winds and usually rain, thunder, lightning, or snow.

> **Chaos /cha·os/:** complete disorder and confusion.

> **Pandemic [pan-dem-ik]:** (of a disease) prevalent throughout an entire country, continent, or the whole world; epidemic over a large area.

These courageous women of color are linking arms, building a legacy, pushing and thriving through the storm and breaking their silence in order to "Leave no Woman Behind."

Join **seven** courageous brave women on the transformational journey to inner-healing and taking their power back by breaking their silence with their stories of emerging. In <u>Becoming Visible,</u> you will experience highs and lows of the Inner-Healing experience. A series of butterfly collections of short, but powerful stories. This is a safe container, a safe space for teens, women of domestic violence, sexual assault, trauma, grief, loss, rejection, teenage pregnancy and codependency to be heard, seen, witnessed and believed so that you can experience recovery and healing. You will experience homelessness, suicide, and mental health stigma. You will discover and learn **seven** principles to help you overcome trauma to transformation.

Stigma: a mark of disgrace associated with a particular circumstance, quality, or person.

HOLLYWOOD FACTS

Let's discuss Hollywood, flashing lights for a minute. I'm going to ask you to review the below list of famous celebrities and think about what they all have in common.

Reese Witherspoon, Halle Berry, Christina Aguilera, Tina Turner, Kerry Washington, Katy Perry, Marilyn Monroe, Selena Gomez, Madonna, Lisa Nichols, Aretha Franklin, Oprah Winfrey, Maya Angelou, Rihanna, Vanessa Laine Bryant

Lisa Nichols and Marilyn Monroe have been diagnosed with dyslexia, a learning disability.

Maya Angelou showed how to survive rape and racism, and still be joyful.

Aretha Franklin was a teen mom at the age of thirteen and married to a pimp at nineteen. She still became the Queen of Soul. Aretha didn't have an easy upbringing. The mom of four became pregnant with her first child when she was just twelve years old. To make the situation even more complicated, Aretha's mother left the family due to her husband's infidelity when Aretha was only six years old, leaving her without a mom to help her navigate the unplanned pregnancy.

Oprah Winfrey's life was full of traumatic experiences. Her family was poor and received welfare benefits. Oprah also endured years of sexual abuse.

The one thing all of these rock star celebrities have in common is they stand up and advocate for one thing, and that is speaking up and standing to unite for domestic violence. This abuse extends past the average American; it affects Hollywood as well. Whether they have experienced directly or indirectly they stand strong by the movement.

These next women know firsthand what it's like to survive domestic violence and become stronger through their pain.

For years, Halle Berry watched her mother fall victim to domestic violence. Berry said, "I saw my mother battered and beaten many years of my life and I felt helpless." She grew up watching her father abuse her mother and older sister and then repeated the pattern in her own life.

In 1993, Berry told Ebony magazine that a boyfriend's beatings had caused her to lose 80 percent of the hearing in her right ear. "The minute he did that, I was gone," she told

The Daily Mail in 2007. "My mother always told me, "If a man hits you, you leave.""

Pop Princess Christina Aguilera has written several songs about her childhood and the domestic abuse that came from her father.

Back in early 2009, Rihanna's performance at the 51st Annual Grammy Awards was canceled due to her now ex-boyfriend Chris Brown beating her. TMZ got a hold of the photos and the word exploded. In 2013, they rekindled their flame. Rihanna is one of the most unforgettable domestic violence survivors. "A lot of women, a lot of young girls, are still going through it. A lot of young boys, too. It's not a subject to sweep under the rug, so I can't just dismiss it like it wasn't anything."

It is no secret about Tina Turner. We watched her story and the things she suffered from in *What's Love Got to Do With It?* In an interview with The Daily Beast, Ike Turner said, "Yeah, I hit her, but I didn't hit her more than an average guy beats his wife." Ike also made her change her name to Tina Turner so that he could always own her. Tina Turner told Oprah, "I never put a lot of praise on myself because of my relationship with Ike. I was just happy when I started to like myself—when I divorced and took control of my life."

Selena Gomez says she experienced emotional abuse in her past relationship with fellow musician Justin Bieber. Gomez first started dating Bieber in 2011 when she was eighteen and he was sixteen. The two musicians last dated in 2018.

My point of sharing these highlights is that through research I discovered proof that no one is exempt from abuse and trauma and you can overcome the struggles and thrive through the storm. Are you ready?

If you or someone you know is a victim of domestic violence, call The National Domestic Violence Hotline at 1-800-799-7233.

Written *with edits by* Marissa Montelongo

Clinical Social Worker and Speaker
Sacramento, CA

Part 1: See Me

Chapter1

Trauma to Transformation
Butterfly Principle: Stop Being a Victim

No one owes you a damn thing, take responsibility on your part. Stop thinking and acting like a victim. Self-care and self-love will allow you the power to set yourself free. Give yourself permission to heal. Free your mind, body and soul.

Princess Warrior
War of Love is Not Battle Scars
By: Nurse Candyce Pirtle-Smalls

S he was sixteen and an inmate at Fairfield, CA Detention Center for the second time. This time was very serious. She sat in the pod area, wearing an oversized blue jumpsuit and secondhand shoes. One hand pressed the telephone to her ear and the other covered her empty ear, cancelling out the background noise.

Her mother's voice was stern and full of tough love, "You better hope he's not dead. You have a 3-month-old baby, you can't spend the rest of your life behind bars for murder." Her heart sank to her stomach. She didn't know what to feel. She was numb.

Battlefield Strength of a Princess Warrior

My mom was thirty when she had me. Three years later, she and my dad divorced. My dad and I kept a strong relationship as I was always daddy's little girl. I was the youngest of three, my siblings well into their teens by the time I was born. As I grew up, I was often left alone with instructions: do not open the door, and if anyone calls your mom is asleep.

My single mom worked hard for our middle class, private school lifestyle. She was a nurse in the ICU and psychiatric ward and a chef at a nightclub. I lived a life of luxury with my own room, lunch money and spending money. I was involved in afterschool programs, tutoring, and was allowed to spend the night at friends' houses. *So why did I often lay in bed at night pleading to God?*

We moved frequently, and I was often "the new kid." Kids at the public school called me "square girl." Maybe it was my thick Steve Urkel glasses, big nose, chipmunk cheeks, or the valley girl tone in my voice. "You sound like a white girl," they'd tease.

I witnessed the domestic violence between my mom and a few of her boyfriends. One time, at the age of five, I saw him slam her forehead against a wooden door—so hard that the smears of her red lipstick were left behind. Her response? She ran into the garage, grabbed a baseball bat and busted the windows of his Mustang.

I was in the fourth grade when another boyfriend jammed her up against the wall and closed his hands around her throat. "Call 911!" My mom yelled, right before telling me to hang up. Fighting and chaos were a nightly ritual. One night when they were both obliterated, he threatened, "I will shoot you and your daughter!"

Tough love was the tool. I learned that love was a verb, an action that hurt. Mommy told me, "If I didn't love you, I wouldn't hit you." Discipline meant slaps to the face, kicks, stomps, vacuum cleaner extension cord to the body, and hand swats.

Love (noun): an intense feeling of deep affection

– Webster's Dictionary

I See You – The Act of Suicide

"You better have your homework done before I get home, or I will kill you!"

Maybe if I die, she'll miss me. I went to the kitchen cabinet, grabbed a random pill bottle and took a handful. As I swallowed the pills, my stomach began to burn. Frustrated that I didn't die, I threw a glass of water on the floor and used a shard to cut my arm. My mom found my 10-year-old body lying on the floor with a bloody arm.

"Girl get your stupid ass up off my floor! Get in the

bathroom and clean up! I'm not going to lose my hospital job playing around with your stupid ass!"

I went to bed and later woke up to a burning hunger. I attempted to fry some pre-rolled lumpia and went to lay down. Smelling the smoke, I realized the kitchen was on fire. *Maybe the job will be done now.*

Four years later, my boyfriend's uncle shared a story in the Vallejo Newspaper about a young girl's mother who stabbed her in her head with an ice pick. Yup, that was me. My mother had a big blow out over her boyfriend sexually harassing me. One night he was drunk and we got into a verbal altercation that caused her to snap. I was pregnant and she wanted me to get an abortion, like she had forced me to do when I was 12 years old. I had always hated her for that. After she reached over and stabbed me several times in my head, I hopped out the car with blood all over my white sweatshirt. I ran into someone's garage, "Help me, my mother tried to kill me and I'm pregnant!" The hospital sent me to live with my older sister. My mom was arrested that night and ordered anger management and parenting classes by the court.

Dear Diary,

We met in July 1998. The fireworks went off for him, an out-of-towner boy who resembled Tupac with his red bandana and nose ring. I was mesmerized by his "thug passion." I was only thirteen and he was seventeen when he swept me off my feet, promising to take care of me and give me shopping sprees.

I lusted and yearned for his affection, putting him before myself. In exchange, I got his forbidden love. He cared about me. He believed in me, and he was the only one in the world who loved me, or so I thought. I was finally seen. Like Bonnie and Clyde, it was us against the world.

He began to manipulate me. He said I was only good for sex and that no one would ever love me, especially if I got fat. He said if I got fat, he'd stay with me, but he wouldn't have sex with me. My first name became "bitch."

He was jealous and insecure. He played on my emotions by looking at other girls in front of me and humiliating me. When around his friends, he'd order me to keep my head down and stay quiet. He did this in front of his mom and family too. People asked, "Why are you treating her like that?" He laughed.

Within months, things got physical. I admit, I'd antagonize him and pick a fight. I'd test him. I thought that if he loved me, he'd hit me. Or, I'd fear getting hit and wanted to see what he'd do. Love was pain and if he didn't hit me then he didn't love me…

Love is patient, love is kind, love is not jealous.

– 1 Corinthians 13:4

When I was 14 years old, my mom got an apartment for us. I was on my way to African dance class one day when he stopped me at the door, accusing my male instructor of wanting to sleep with me. I tried to leave, and he pushed me so hard into the wall that my back went through and left an imprint.

I ran to the kitchen and grabbed a block of knives to throw at him. Next thing I knew, I was on the ground. I pulled myself up, ran into the bathroom and locked the door. I looked in the mirror and saw his shoe print on my forehead. Fear paralyzed me. I went into the walk-in closet, closed the door, and curled into a ball.

"Candyce, what happened to the wall?"

"I tripped over the rug, Mommy, and fell."

"Yeah ok, y'all better not be fighting and carrying on."

I had to tell more lies and it was humiliating. In the ninth grade, I was playing my Spice Girls CD and he became enraged, so he pinned me on the ground and broke the CD over my face and attempted to make me eat the CD. The next day at school, my friends saw the scratches on my face and creases on the corners of my mouth. They asked me what happened. I made up a story.

He got me pregnant. I was determined to keep my baby. This was a planned pregnancy, and we were so happy. *I wanted a baby so bad. I wanted someone to love me.*

One day he attacked my mom, pinning her to the bed, holding a pillow over her head and punching her. "Candyce, help me, helllp me!" I stood there paralyzed, playing his manipulation in my head: *she doesn't love you.* My mom told my gangster uncle about it and he hid under our bed one night, scaring us out of the house. That night my abuser kept me awake, telling me that if I blinked, he'd slap me and make me lick the bottom of his shoe.

My grades had slipped as he often forced me to skip class for him. Eventually dropping out, he had me all to himself. We slept in his incarcerated father's abandoned van, parked in the projects of the city. He would gaslight, or psychologically abuse me, to the point of questioning my sanity. One day he left and when he returned, he tortured me saying I'd been spotted with another guy. He squeezed my fresh nose and ear piercings together to cause me pain and keep me in agony. Pure evil, just pure evil. I cried and pleaded until he apologized and admitted to his lie. He would spit on me and tell me I was worthless.

It tore my parents' heart out knowing their daughter was homeless with her dangerous boyfriend. I sold drugs for him on one occasion and got a gun pulled out on me. My dad sent me money and told me, "If you truly loved yourself, you wouldn't let him manipulate you." My mom pleaded, "Candyce, we miss you, please come home."

I had my own room waiting for me, but on one condition: I returned without him.

***

Question: How did you muster the courage to break away from the relationship? What advice can you share with someone who says she is afraid and doesn't have the emotional strength to leave?

Answer: *Have you ever seen stars before? He knocked me out one day with one hit. I fell into the fence outside. It was dark and his uncle just made a pass at me for me to leave him and be with him. I always thought he hit me with an open hand, and now I think he must have hit me with a closed fist as the power and force knocked me to the ground.*

Fast forward, I had just birthed my son. Although I lacked self-love, I couldn't allow my son to witness the toxicity. The abuse continued after I had my baby. He slapped me with my baby in my hand, and another day, I didn't make the baby's bottle to his liking, so he punched me in my head while I was laying down with the baby. If he would have missed, he would have hit my baby. I knew that the toxic relationship was getting worse. I remember warning his mom that either I was going to kill her son or he was going to kill me.

It actually ended with him lying on the floor begging for

help as I stood over him with a knife in my hand. He had financially abused me, humiliated me, and hit me in public for the last time. "I hope you die," I said.

He was airlifted to John Muir Hospital, and I was left with a 3-month-old baby, sitting in Juvenile Hall. I knew it was time. I was at my limit and I just wanted out of the whirlwind of my addiction.

My advice for anyone experiencing relationship violence is to reach out and talk to someone. Start the exit process of secretly taking photos of texts, photos, journal and reach out to someone you trust. Safety comes first. My goal is for you not to determine your past with your future. You never know who you will grow up to be. Spread awareness.

Author's Note on Forgiveness

It took a while for my mother and I to replenish our relationship. I called her one day and forgave her for all the pain and underlying hatred I had for her. I apologized for my disrespect and pain I caused her. No matter our differences, my mother never gave up on me. Her love was tough love and it made me into the woman I was becoming. We now have a beautiful bond, the best relationship a girl could ever imagine. I learned that a person can't give you what they don't have to give you. You must find love within yourself. Growing up, I don't remember my mom verbally telling me she loved me. Later I found out my mother's mom never told her that she loved her. Generations of pain we must break.

My story is a bit different than the usual story heard of DV. I'm a survivor of teenage DV. I found my power in rebelling with food. I was able to shift my habits and gain control over my life by losing fifty pounds of teenage pregnancy, resentment, shame, lies, excuses and lack of self-care and self-love. I kept the pain off by meal prepping. Overachieving and my type-A personality ensured I'd be successful. Becoming a teenage mom at the age of sixteen to my now soon-to-be 20-year-old son was a beautiful recipe for failure.

Family members whispered about me, thinking I would never amount to become anything or anyone. Or that I would fall victim to statistics and become uneducated, on street drugs, live on welfare and have multiple children with multiple men.

I proved the world wrong. I proved the chatter wrong.

Growing up in a toxic environment and witnessing dysfunction, chaos, rage and explosive behaviors, the odds were definitely against me. As I transformed physically, mentally, and spiritually, God my heavenly Father in Christ, has shown me this story isn't my story. It is a story that needs to be shared all over the world in order to heal other women's inner pain by showing them the light Jesus Christ.

Today, I provide women a safe space to be heard, seen and believed as they dive into their inner healing. We discuss eating habits and how mindless eating is a behavior and habit of subconsciously coping with inner hidden trauma. As we peel back the onion layers, we discover their wounds. Women have been successful and move into a beautiful journey of self-discovery.

Let's Reflect Workbook Activity

1. Who do you need to forgive in your past or present?

   _____

2. What were some emotions Candyce was lacking as a kid?

   _____

3. What were some emotions you lacked as a kid?

   _____

4. What were some red flags that the relationship you just read about was a toxic and abusive relationship rather than healthy? List 4 examples.

   _____

5. Define self-love and self-care and why it is important for you.

   _____

Who am I?

Candyce Pirtle-Smalls is a Nurse, Educator, Speaker, Health/Life Coach, and 2x Bestselling Author of <u>Mindful Meal Prep: Clean, Delicious Recipes for Weight Loss</u>.

She beat the statistics and is an educator with teaching credentials from U.C. Berkley and a nurse of ten years with a degree in Science of Nursing. Candyce works in management as a mental health nurse for adolescents. She's an entrepreneur with a successful career of coaching and a global public motivational speaker. She's the CEO of Fit in Her Kitchen, LLC and the Founder/Executive Director of F.I.T. Butterfly Innovation Inc. She is me. I am her. "Don't give up on yourself, you never know who you are becoming."

Please visit my sites for information on my workshops, referrals, and how to work with my organizations.

Website: <u>www.nursecandysmalls.com</u>

<u>www.fitbutterfly.org</u>

Contact Information:

Non-Profit Email: info@fitbutterfly.org

Instagram: @fit_butterfly_innovation

@nursecandy_healtheducator

Facebook:

https://www.facebook.com/Fit-Butterfly-Innovation-Inc-111521143930911/ **Join our movement, send a private message for access to our private group!**

LinkedIn:

https://www.linkedin.com/incandyce-pirtle-smalls-lvn-36560a13a

Mailing Address:

1990 N. California Blvd Suite 20 Walnut Creek, CA. 94596

Signs of abuse: unexpected bouts of anger or rage, unusual moodiness, pressuring a partner into unwanted sexual activity, being blamed for problems in the relationship, a partner who doesn't take responsibility for their actions, controlling tendencies, explosive temper, socially isolating you, constantly monitoring your whereabouts and checking in to see what you are doing and who you are with, falsely accusing you, vandalizing or ruining your personal property, taunting or bullying, threatening or causing physical violence

If your partner frequently engages in these behaviors it may be wise to speak with someone whom you feel comfortable with. Adults who have experience with relationships may be able to provide advice that can help you to determine if you are in any danger.

Teen dating violence: the physical, sexual, or psychological/emotional abuse within a dating relationship among adolescents. Intimate partner violence has been a well examined and documented phenomenon in adults. However, there has not been nearly as much study on violence in adolescent dating relationships and it is therefore not as well understood. The research has mainly focused on

Caucasian youth and there are yet no studies which focus specifically on Intimate Partner Violence (IPV) in adolescent same-sex romantic relationships.

The current statistics on teen dating violence tell a scary story: **One in 10 teen girls and one in 11 teen boys** admit to having experienced physical violence in a dating relationship in the past year. One in three teens say they know someone who has been physically assaulted or hurt by a dating partner.

Teen Pregnancy

In 2017, a total of 194,377 babies were born to women aged 15-19 years, for a birth rate of 18.8 per 1,000 women in this age group. This is another record low for U.S. teens and a drop of 7% from 2016. Birth rates fell 10% for women aged 15-17 years and 6% for women aged 18-19 years.

Teen pregnancy and childbearing bring substantial social and economic costs through immediate and long-term impacts on teen parents and their children.

- Pregnancy and birth are significant contributors to high school dropout rates among girls. Only about 50% of teen mothers receive a high school diploma by 22 years of age, whereas approximately 90% of women who do not give birth during adolescence graduate from high school.

- The children of teenage mothers are more likely to have lower school achievement and to drop out of high school, have more health problems, be incarcerated at some time during adolescence, give birth as a teenager, and face unemployment as a young adult.

- On a positive note, between 1991 and 2015, the teen birth rate dropped to 64%, which resulted in $4.4 billion in public savings in 2015 alone.

I Soulify Episode 15: Use self-love and mindfulness to break the emotional bonds of domestic violence. This episode is now streaming in five different countries including the U.S. I invite you to listen to see how I have broken the generational bonds of trauma and healing through mindful eating! Be sure to tune in. I would love to hear your feedback.

https://podcasts.apple.com/us/podcast/isoulify-podcast/id1466117576

It was an absolute honor to be interviewed on the I Soulify Podcast, speaking on domestic violence and inner healing to five countries, including the U.S.

Credits:

Hair: D'Mara Latrice Hair Salon, San Jose, CA

IG: @styylez_by_dmara_beautyfiend

Wardrobe Stylist: Charleszetta Baldwin AKA "Charlie on the Spot," Oakland, CA

IG: @charlie_onthespot

Makeup Artist: Irene Robinson, Pittsburg, CA (East Bay)

IG: @iro.makeup

Email: iro.makeup7@gmail.com

Chapter 2

Trauma to Transformation
Butterfly Principle: The Act of Giving and Receiving

"Forgive myself for everything, including my participation."

What does the lonely heart do when it's broken? By:
Teisha Y. Levi

The smell of weed filled the tiny one-bedroom apartment. That stench, the molded windowpanes and inadequate air flow were enough to stir up some anxiety. I laid on my bed and considered the long ride to the city. My morning routine included dropping him off before my class. Any conflict with him always ended in physical pain, so I decided not to bring it up. I knew he had once again cheated on me.

He asked me a question. I was busy and ignored him. I felt his presence behind me but didn't turn around. Fear fell upon me. I turned to him, but before I could speak, he pushed me against the wall and tightened his hands around my throat, demanding an answer. I attempted to scream, which only made matters worse. I was thrown to the floor and repeatedly kicked in my stomach and chest. I reached for the edge of the counter and managed to pull myself up. I scrambled to the kitchen, feeling his rage behind me. Out of fear, I closed my eyes and began feeling around for a shield. The ancient knife set was right at my fingertips. Sounds of chaos rang from the apartment and moments later I was handcuffed and lugged away.

He was the "cool guy" and made me laugh at first

sight. He'd occasionally remind me that he had always wanted a girl like me, loyal and smart. He brought the experiences, both good and bad. But the night before, the percentage of his profit didn't meet his expectations nor match his efforts of posting on the block all day. He was sensitive when it came to money. I never really understood the risk related to his work and I never asked because I knew he would only oppose.

I felt worthless. I was afraid and voiceless. I felt unappreciated and yet, I still gave. But despite the darkness around me, a glimmer of light shone on my educational journey. I did my best to stay focused even though I was suffering. Emotionally, I was numb. Mentally, I was drained. I was wasting away due to my lack of appetite, and I physically mirrored an ill patient. People knew, people assumed, but no one asked. I was in a sunken depression.

There are cold and lonely places some may never see. The seventy-two hours spent in county jail taught me a valuable lesson: no one is immune to negative consequences, not even the young girl with dreams, so it's imperative that in the face of adversity we choose to thrive. I was determined to push through my education. I tackled a full college course-load while working forty to fifty hours a week. That became my life. After a few years, I decided to take a month off from everything in order to gain insight as to who I was and what I was working towards. It amazes me that despite my circumstances, I never lost connection with my goals.

I left him and it wasn't easy. Protecting myself meant long nights and hard days of torment and chase. My refusal to acknowledge him only fed his rage. He waited outside my job for my shift to end at midnight*. He left threatening messages on my supervisor's voicemail. I continued to distract myself with work and school. I was determined to be the first in my immediate family to graduate college and I carried the obligation to be an illustration of propensity for those I encountered. As a child, my mother said, "No one can ever take away what you have learned, so get an education." My parents had both taught me the principles of trial and adversity.

Growing up, I witnessed dysfunctional family behaviors; my first example of family discord. The family code was to never discuss what happened inside our home. We were programmed to keep our business out of public knowledge. Therefore, I kept my silence.

Most family violence occurs behind closed doors, and no family is guaranteed immunity. Family violence does not discriminate against social class, ethnicity, race or gender. Researchers have attempted to understand what exactly constitutes family violence and its prevalence. However, data collection is difficult due to individuals' failure to either acknowledge or report abusive behavior.

***

Writing helped save my life. I quickly discovered the therapeutic power of thoughts on paper. No other set of eyes could read my pain, thus shielding me from outside judgment. It was *my* story. Writing bore feelings I never admitted before. Out of desire to reconstruct my personal self and values, I no longer wanted to hide behind anguish. That thirst led me to the discovery of self-love through the art of forgiveness. With the support of a mental health therapist, I began to practice honesty and transparency. I was unaware that by practicing forgiveness, I'd have the opportunity to revisit and reflect on my past experiences and choices. My past experiences became lessons to share with other brave souls.

As I continued to unpack and accept my experiences, I realized that I had participated in my own victimization by staying after the first physical altercation. I accepted being devalued and unappreciated. I hadn't been honest with myself and it was time for accountability. I learned how to be kind to myself. I developed empathy for those who participated in my experiences. A common saying became a realization: *hurt people, hurt people.*

The "cool guy" was a victim of child abandonment, sexual abuse and a witness to community violence. He had shared pieces of his story with me but was hesitant to use his voice and avoided opportunities for true healing. He either numbed his pain with substances or inflicted it onto others, like me. My codependent personality allowed submission to this dysfunctional arrangement, and like many other young women who are voiceless and silenced, I never spoke publicly until now.

I was first introduced to the world of public speaking several years ago while hosting a podcast called *Healing and Empowerment*, where complex topics such as family crisis and self-love were discussed. Although I touched on topics of healing, I hadn't fully emerged from the shadows of my own truth. I continued this practice of using my voice and speaking from my experiences while teaching a college course entitled <u>Family Crisis: Codependency and Substance Use</u>. Some called it coincidence, but I called it fate, allowing another opportunity to be visible. Currently, I continue to share my skills and educate by leading a group of associates who are pending official licensure as mental health professionals.

A trauma to transformation principle that guides my healing is *"forgive myself for everything, including my participation."* As a tool for your own healing, I urge you to consider this principle. Recognize what blocks you from healing and work on releasing it. Challenge yourself to identify every person and situation that has ever taken your power. Document any negative thoughts and feelings then counteract them by writing affirming and empathic thoughts. This process is the *transformation* to your healing.

Counseling and psychotherapy can have both risks and benefits. Therapy includes discussions of your personal challenges and difficulties, which can elicit uncomfortable feelings, such as sadness, guilt, anger and frustration. However, counseling has been shown to have many benefits related to personal growth. Counseling can often lead to better interpersonal relationships, improved academic performance, solutions to specific problems and reductions in your feelings of distress related to the traumatic experience. There is no assurance of these benefits without active participation. This process may seem complex and considerably vulnerable, but the personal transformation will be gratifying.

Although I will never forget what I've been through, I can confidently say that I have evolved. I've gained knowledge about myself and my purpose, which is: to shift generational dysfunction of families by spreading awareness about domestic and intimate partner violence. I no longer fear dysfunction because I have the courage and ability to effectively articulate my thoughts and feelings. I am a woman of color who has participated in my own pain and was once not brave enough to ask for help. I am a Black woman who fell victim to family and intimate partner violence**. I am a leader, survivor, therapist, sister and friend.

Today, I consciously construct natural shifts in choices. I have fewer toxic interactions and experiences because I live with more positive intentions. My past has been rough, but my healing has been tougher. The more personal work I did, the more obtainable my goals became. I am now a Licensed Marriage and Family Therapist and serve other people of color facing challenges of unresolved trauma that affect their ability to live a meaningful life. Many of these individuals have a story just like mine. Individuals who have experienced and survived dysfunctional patterns and intimate partner violence often feel a sense of neglect, guilt, and abandonment that leads to their silence. Oftentimes they will experience fear and judgement, which can be a personal challenge in seeking support.

Mary, a 24-year-old woman has been taught by her parents that you stay with your partner for better or worse. What does worse even mean? How "bad" is "too bad?" She knows that being hit is wrong and her relationship is a mess. But she believes she must stay and make it better. What we see here is family dysfunctional beliefs, shame, guilt, and self-doubt. What is also true here is that violence affects people in different ways and changes them forever. These individuals often experience elevated symptoms of anxiety, post-traumatic stress disorder (PTSD), and depression. The importance of therapy is crucial in helping to live a violence-free life with guidance and support in avoiding further victimization. Does this resonate with you? Do your family beliefs and dynamics serve you? Are you ready to evolve in healthier ways?

As the reader, my goal is for you to develop empathy for yourself and your experiences. You may ask yourself: *Can I heal? When will I get over it? How can I change behaviors that do not serve me in order to emerge into who I am destined to be?*

Challenge yourself to do the work and reflect on your own journey in order to make the shift to transformation. The principle of forgiveness will foster empathy and the understanding that personal failures are simply opportunities for healing. Our emotional and physical pains are all indications that something must be released in order for something new to emerge!

***

If you or someone you know is facing a mental health crisis, please reach out to your local city or county resource line for therapy referrals and crisis resources. Dial 911 or go to the nearest emergency room.

Please visit www.mentalwellnesswithteisha.com for resources and inquiries regarding therapy referrals to other Mental Health Professionals in the Bay Area, CA.

References:

1. Resources and Institutional knowledge – National Clearinghouse of Defense of Battered Women and Battered Women's Justice Project
2. O. Barnett, C. Miller-Perrin, R. Perrin., *Family Violence Across the Lifespan*. Second Edition. 2005.

Let's Reflect Workbook Activity

1. How can I change dysfunctional family behaviors and beliefs?

   _____

2. Can and will I ever heal from past pain and trauma?

   _____

3. How can you forgive when you can never forget?

   _____

4. Have I experienced ruptures in my attachment with others, specifically with my parents or caretakers?

   _____

5. What are ways I love and value myself?

   _____

6. What are ways I imagine my story can help other survivors find their voice?

   _____

About Teisha

Teisha Y. Levi, Licensed Marriage and Family Therapist #101104, is based in the Bay Area region of Oakland, California. Teisha introduced herself to the world of public speaking several years ago, hosting her own podcast called Healing and Empowerment via Radio Podcast discussing complex topics like Family Crisis and the Power of Forgiveness, while completing her professional education and training in the field of Counseling Psychology. Now licensed, Teisha currently works in direct care as she also operates a private therapy practice, Mental Wellness with Teisha, located in Oakland, CA.

Teisha also leads with experience in teaching a family crisis and co-dependency course for two years, at San Francisco State University in San Francisco, offering knowledge in the area of family crisis, resilience and coping. She teaches undergraduate level upper-division students with a primary focus on mental health and substance use. Teisha currently spends her time leading weekly supervision groups for interns working to complete LMFT/LCSW licensure in California. Teisha also manages a small caseload of private clients while working at a local hospital as a licensed therapist in the psychiatry department.

Teisha works with a wide range of emotional,

cognitive, and behavioral issues providing experienced therapy in the areas of depression, anxiety, trauma, grief, anger management, and serious mental illnesses. "It's been extremely rewarding to support those who struggle with their painful past, or who turn to the emotion of anger, and who are vested in the unwillingness to forgive, I can help change that perspective," wrote Teisha.

As Co-Author of Becoming Visible: Emerging to Greater Heights Vol. 1, Teisha uses her passion of writing to emerge the reader into a personal space of vulnerability, a story of trauma to transformation. The purpose is to empower other women who suffer from intimate partner violence to fight through the storm in order to evolve into the butterfly they are destined to be.

Credits:

Hair Stylist: Iesha Burks of San Leandro (Braider)

Email: dimples12272002@yahoo.com

Makeup Artist: Felicia B. of San Leandro, CA.

(510) 707-1491

Wardrobe: Self

Contact Information:

Teisha Y. Levi, Licensed Marriage and Family Therapist #101104

Email: teishalevi@gmail.com

Website: www.mentalwellnesswithteisha.com

IG: @mentalwellnesswithteisha

Location: Bay Area, CA. (Counties: Alameda, Contra Costa, San Francisco)

*Among adult victims of rape, physical violence, and/or stalking by an intimate partner, 22% of women and 15% of men first experienced some form of partner violence between 11 and 17 years of age (National Center for Injury Prevention and Control Division of Violence Prevention.)

**Intimate partner violence and abuse are the terms used for violence and abuse that occur between adult partners who are at least 18-years-old, sexually intimate, married or unmarried, and currently or formerly living together." Family Violence Across the Lifespan, O. Barnett, C. Miller-Perrin, R. Perrin. Second Edition (pg. 251.)

Chapter 3

Trauma to Transformation
Butterfly Principle: Self-Value

The regard that something is held to deserve; the importance, worth, or usefulness of something. A sense of one's own value as a human being: feeling of self-worth or self-esteem.

Value Me

By: Ericka Parker

S he was favored – a princess in a home filled with love and security. Living in a small California town where everyone knew her name. A last name that had a good reputation. A last name that blazed the trail for her first job, her acceptance in select circles and the expectation of a certain level of behavior. Growing up the youngest of four siblings, there were different behaviors that she felt she could have mimicked.

Perhaps the most impressionable of behaviors came from her two ambitious and hardworking parents. They were a God-fearing couple with strong financial discipline that landed their family in an upper middle-class neighborhood where opportunities were limitless. They had humble beginnings growing up in the country sticks of East Texas. They worked hard and became successful from nothing, thriving as a family living in California. The environment was conducive for success and all the luxuries to be content and live stress-free for a child growing up.

While she was constantly told that she was strong, she felt weak. She was praised for being confident, yet she felt intimidated often. She was told she was fearless, yet she felt afraid and lonely. She knew the bible scriptures but did not apply them to her life. The most dominant belief that she held was her insecurity of being brown-skinned. The images on TV and in magazines were opposite from her. She was never vocal or emotional about it, but deep down she did not believe she was pretty. Dreams of being a shade lighter with light eyes and long hair plagued her thoughts. To compensate, she excelled at being outgoing, active and the life of the party.

Her first love was predictable on both ends. He was the one everyone approved of and all believed they were a match made in "puppy love" heaven. They had known each other since they were little children. He came from a good home, similar family structure and was part of her church circle. A nice young man who was respectful and a stand-out athlete in baseball and basketball. He was a hopeless romantic, kind-hearted and very safe for her. All that he was contributed to the making of a good story. He adored her and she was secure in his arms. The hometown hero and church darling were the ultimate High School Sweethearts.

The shift occurred when *that boy* moved into town. A mysterious new kid whose father transferred to the military base from Japan. That boy was smooth, a phenomenal basketball player with quick wit. He was not book smart, but extremely street smart. He was charming with the ladies and had a bad boy edge that was intriguing. That boy's eyes were fastened on her and she fawned over him for more than a year until all his attempts were on the table.

We call him *that boy* because this was the name her mother chose to call him as she spotted danger right away. "Why is that boy calling you so much?" mother would ask. "That boy is up to no good."

She was confused with emotions and raging with hormones at the age of sixteen. That boy was fun and edgy— there were adventures with all their encounters. Finally, after months of flirting with each other that boy convinced her to be his new love. That boy wrote letters, he recited poetry, and drew her pictures expressing his undying love. She felt alive with that boy and grown, like she wanted to be, not playing kid games as she felt accustomed. The church girl life and pretending to honor her upbringing was exhausting for her. She just wanted to live free.

As she got closer to that boy there was a wedge that formed between her and the family. There were fights with her mother who could sense that trouble was erupting. That boy used his words to be an influence on her but not for the good. That boy influenced her to do things she never would have dared to do. She was blinded by his charisma; his incredible talent was exciting. The attention that he would receive from everyone made her feel like the queen bee on campus. Other girls were envious of her and she loved it.

While that boy had all those things going for him, he had a temper and jealous side underneath. That boy convinced her that his temper and aggression was her fault because he was so in love. If anyone came between this, he would destroy them. After a couple years of being together, the love was fading in the background of the lies, disappointments, cheating, and head games. The dramatic break ups and then make ups. The dysfunctional mood swings made her senior year of high school miserable. College life was beginning, and she was deeply depressed.

That boy's basketball journey to a Division 1 college did not go the way he planned and the way everyone expected with his great talent. He was playing basketball at the junior college level with aspirations to progress forward. But at the age of nineteen and a half, he had become an afterthought to all the good teams, and the potential of a flourishing career was completely bleak. That boy drank so much lately and was full of ego that was not being fulfilled. Every day there was an accusation that she was cheating, that she was lying, or that she didn't really love him. The energy it took for her to reassure that boy that she was down for him was exhausting. The intimidation and mind games were draining but she stayed anyway, looking for opportunities and thinking of a plan to end this relationship.

One winter weekend after spending an entire day together alone in that boy's parents' home, a scene erupted that was like a Lifetime movie. While that boy was occupied on the phone in another room, she spotted a letter folded underneath his lamp. With each unfold of the paper, a lump swelled deeper and deeper in her throat. As if she knew once again the contents of the document. Another love note from an admiring fan–some poor girl pouring out her heart and frustration. Maybe it was another friend of hers who felt so torn about being the side piece. It had become a reoccurring episode from a bad flick.

The letter was from someone whom she considered an acquaintance. Not a friend because her circle had become so small over the last two years. Her real friends had begun to distance themselves, as everyone who cared for her was frustrated that she could not see that boy for who he really was. They felt she was brainwashed and stupid for dealing with him. New girls would become friendly to her as they were setting up for an attack. The true desire was to be around that boy and steal her man.

A fast scan of the letter and her eyes locked onto five words: *I'm six months pregnant now!* She dropped the letter and quickly went into a panic attack. That boy was still on the phone in the living room. She was enraged and seeing red! Her hormones were raging, and the anger had overtaken her. This was it! The ultimate betrayal, the final straw, and she was ready to walk away. In her mind played scenes of nights when she could not get in touch with him and weekends when he didn't come home from college two hours away. Times when he would say he fell asleep and didn't call her back. Then, at that very moment, she began to remember how just hours ago she told that boy she was eight weeks pregnant and they were making plans.

Since they were both out of high school now and she was over eighteen they decided they would marry, and that boy would go into the Army so they could become a family. She remembered this right at the moment when she was looking quickly for an object from the kitchen on her way to the living room. Suddenly her feet stopped moving and she was stuck as she overheard that boy say on the phone, "I love her not you and I'm getting married!"

As if under a hypnotic spell after overhearing this, she turned around and walked quickly back into the bedroom. She grabbed the letter, folded it back in the same pattern she found it and placed it underneath the lamp. A few seconds later she found herself in the bathroom standing in front of the mirror crying silently so he would not hear. Her heart was racing; she could see it literally beat upon her chest. Her face looked distorted and she began to vomit. As she washed her face with cool water, the reflection in the mirror looked unfamiliar. She was looking at a stranger. The joy was gone from her eyes. The innocence of love was muddy. The heaviness had taken a toll on her heart.

That boy knocked on the door – "Hey, are you okay? You've been in there a long time!" She had been there a long time, nearly three years to be exact. Was she okay? If okay meant that this time she had finally made the decision to take responsibility for her actions. If okay meant that her decision to come correct to her parents and face the music of being with a child. If okay meant she would stand up to him and say no more! Then yes, she was okay! This was the final dance—no more deception, no more lies, no more manipulation and no more drama!

She walked out of the bathroom and went into his room to grab her bag and car keys to leave. That boy reached around her waist to pull her closer to him. That boy whispered in her ear, "I love you!" That boy gently kissed her neck and began to pull at her clothes. Her head was aching and her eyes burning with anger. Somehow, she found the courage to turn around and look him in the eye and tell him the truth she knew. The truth she had known for a long time—that he was a liar, a womanizer and that she was done! She screamed at the top of her lungs at him and said all the things that were really going on in her heart. It's true that out of the heart the mouth speaks. She said things to him that she never heard herself speak out loud. Hateful words from a place of anger and bitterness. That boy stood there speechless and when she was finished, she pushed him in his chest as hard as she could and turned away to leave.

As she turned to gather her belongings and walk out of the door, that boy grabbed her in the back of her hair and pulled her down to the ground. He jumped on top of her and began to hit her in the face. He put both hands on her throat and began to choke her. She was scratching him and pounding on his forearms. He released the grip on her neck. She scrambled to get from underneath him. That boy continued to restrain her arms as she fluttered to hit him. That boy then grabbed her in the face and threatened to kill her. That boy went into a fit of rage and snapped. As they tousled and physically swabbed, he began to shout at her. Rambling and crying. Tussling with her and holding her down. Kissing her then cursing at her. Ripping her clothes and forcing himself sexually on her. That boy was out of control. This terror went on for what seemed like an hour. That boy finally removed himself looking remorseful and broken. He crawled over to the corner of the room and cried like a 5-year-old.

Her body was numb and her spirit broken. Not only this, but she felt chains holding her down; the weight of them caused her head to bow with shame. She lay there in disgust wondering how she would get away. What was the next move? She cried out, "Jesus, help me get away from this boy!" It is true when the bible declares that the name of the Lord is a strong tower, the righteous run in and are safe.

She was able to remove herself from the terror and make it safely home and then back to school without anyone in her family knowing all the trauma she had been put through. The ability to mask her feelings was a specialty for her. She had become like a character in her own theatrical play. She had become accustomed to giving people what they expected from her and not deviating from the script. The mask, like the covering of a mouth to shield from infection, was also designed by her to shield her from accountability. To cover up hurt, to cover up poor choices, and to cover up shame.

The desperate prayer to Jesus while lying on the floor began to move all over her situation. Over the next five weeks came a series of events that only the Lord was exposing. Her answer for help would come in the most peculiar way. Being honest was empowering for her. There was no more deception as she shared everything that was going on. Her family gave her love, her friends gave her courage. Then a trip to the doctor for her first prenatal appointment would lead to being rushed in an ambulance to the hospital for an emergency ectopic surgery of her fallopian tube. According to the OB/GYN she was in jeopardy of an eruption that could have been life threatening. The life inside was killing her and unable to survive.

When she came to her senses, she could feel the chains being broken and God had set her free. You need to understand now that "She" is me and I am a survivor of my own enemy. The enemy of low self-esteem and feeling unworthy. The enemy of low expectations and fear. In my lowest point I was reminded that if I just called on the name of the Lord, he would come to my rescue. Even in my own created web of destruction, God loved me enough to bring me back to life. To show me my worth and that no situation had to be a permanent condition.

There is an attack from the enemy and oftentimes (not always) the enemy is in you. The enemy in your soul who wants to self-sabotage, self-destruct and self-absorb your future outcome. Your life matters and having a good life matters to the Creator. This is the reason why he exists.

John 10:10 says: *The enemy comes to steal, kill and*

destroy. But I (God) come that you might have life and have it more abundantly.

I encourage you reading this today to understand that your current situation or what you have struggled with is not too hard for God to rescue you from.

Butterfly Principle - Prayer

Prayer is an act of surrendering your heart and desires to God and aligning your will to his divine direction. The dictionary defines the word pray as a verb meaning: to address a solemn request or expression of thanks to a deity or other object of worship.

Declare this prayer over yourself:

Lord, I know that you created me and you love me. You see my worth and while I may not at this very moment, I ask that you empower me to see. Open my eyes and my heart to receive your love and walk in your strength. I surrender to you and trust you to transform my life. In Jesus name, Amen.

Butterfly Principle: Self -Value

The regard that something is held to deserve; the importance, worth, or usefulness of something. A sense of one's own value as a human being: feeling of self-worth or self-esteem.

Declare this proclamation over yourself:

I am beautiful and wonderfully made in my own skin.

I have purpose, destiny and a voice in this world.

My choices are important as they shape my future.

I can overcome any obstacle - no situation is too hard to come out of!

Another person will not ascribe my worth - I am worthy because God says that I am!

Let's Reflect Workbook Activity

1. What do you like about yourself? What are you good at or what are you proud of?

    _____

2. What are things that you like to do or places you like to visit that bring you joy?

    _____

3. Who, around you, doesn't bring out the best in you, but instead the worst?

    _____

4. How can you begin to distance yourself from those who don't make you feel good about yourself?

    _____

5. Who can keep you accountable for your personal development?

    _____

About Ericka Parker

A wife, a mother, career & life coach, a speaker, an entrepreneur and a Pastor! She is compassionate about seeing individuals free from bondage and walking in their purpose. Ericka is affectionately nicknamed "PEP" by those she serves, and the name is characteristic of the energy, encouragement, and ability to motivate all those around her.

Founder of Iron Sharp Consulting, LLC that provides talent acquisition to organizations on a contract basis and professional development to individuals who desire career guidance and transitional help.

Ericka is also the founder of PEPTalk Women's Conference that hosts empowerment sessions, networking, and conferences for women in leadership.

For booking contact www.peptalkconference.com
IG: erickaparker7 or peptalkconferences
Facebook: Ericka Parker
ericka@ironsharpconsulting.com

"SisterHood"

Part 2: Hear Me

Chapter 4

Butterfly Principle Trauma to Transformation: Forgiveness

Forgiving myself and others was a key element along my transformational journey.

"You're Stupid! You're Stupid!"
- My Mother

By: Charleszetta Baldwin "Charlie on the Spot"

The hurtful words still stain my memories. She nearly killed my confidence. There was a time when I really did believe I was stupid. I really did believe she was right about me.

Abuse isn't something that's painted over someone's skin for all to see. You can't see it just by looking through my Instagram or modeling photos. You won't be able to see it when I smile or tell you about my day. But when I was a kid, abuse played a bigger role than hopscotch and Jolly Ranchers.

My mom abused me. There was the physical abuse—she'd pull and slang me around on the kitchen floor. I'll never forget the time she hit me in the head with a payphone at a telephone booth. But more than that, she emotionally abused me, like when she made me sit outside in the dark backyard. According to a 1997 study conducted by Australian Institute of Family Studies, emotional abuse can be more negatively impactful than physical abuse.

As a teenager, I realized that my mother was unhappy. Her pain trickled down onto me. The moment she became frustrated or angry, I became her scapegoat. And when her pain subsided, she apologized. But the apology wasn't really an apology; it was the calm before the storm. The peace never lasted long, because she'd become angry again and the pain-apology cycle would continue.

When I'd leave for school in the morning, I'd try to set aside her painful words. But often, they'd follow me to class, sit on my shoulder and whisper in my ear while I tried to focus. I developed problems with concentrating, understanding the material and keeping track of my assignments. As a result, I fell behind in class, which only led to more anger and more frustration. I became lost.

There was a lack of educational support in both my home and the school system. Without the support, I wasn't really motivated to learn. I used to hate reading aloud. Once I had a teacher who approached me before class and said with a sarcastic giggle, "Charleszetta, you don't know how to read?" I blamed myself for not being able to perform well in school. I mislabeled myself as "stupid" and I believed it for about seventeen years of my life.

Despite the trauma of the emotional abuse, I continued to push forward. I knew that education was the key to bettering myself. I wanted to obtain a degree, and I knew that I'd only be able to do so if I could find a way to retain what was being taught. It wasn't until I enrolled in the College of Alameda and failed English for the third time that I discovered I have dyslexia. It was a make or break, and I was about to lose all of my financial aid for failing my classes. For the first time, I sought help from a counselor.

Looking back on it, I had all of the symptoms of a learning disability. All throughout my schooling, I struggled with reading aloud, pronouncing words and solving arithmetic problems. It was difficult for me to understand sequences of actions and basic expressions. There I was calling myself "stupid" when in reality, I just require a different method of teaching in order to understand and retain the information. All of those years of embarrassment should have been met with comfort and support. I should have received a helping hand instead of a slap on my face.

As soon I discovered that I have dyslexia, I got connected with the systems in place to assist me. I received a generous amount of support through Programs and Services for Students with Disabilities. I was so excited to receive resources such as: personal tutors, audiobooks and more test-taking time. I realized that I could pass my classes and be successful. It was as if someone flipped a switch on in my mind. I was open. I was knowledgeable, and I felt myself rebuilding my confidence.

I was no longer a victim of my environment; I became a survivor! With each day, I felt myself releasing my mother's words and finding inspiration in the positivity I felt. I received my associate degree and Fashion Certificate in Apparel Design and Merchandising. Then, I transferred to California State East Bay where I earned my bachelor's degree in Sociology.

The more I discovered my potential, the more eager I was to share it with the world. I always had a love for fashion and modeling, but it seemed that opportunities were far beyond my reach, literally. I was constantly told that I was too short or that I didn't have the right look, which always led to disappointment and a reevaluation of who I was. For a moment, I accepted it as my fate, allowing the naysayers to dictate which opportunities I chose to pursue.

Then I remembered how I overcame the abuse of my childhood. I remembered how I was able to earn my fashion certificate, associate degree and bachelor's degree—all while having a learning disability. The only thing standing in my way was me! I was my biggest obstacle. I learned that I am the only one who can limit my abilities.

I decided to pursue modeling on my own. I learned poses, photography angles and fashionable looks. I created my own platform in order to pursue my passion. It was because I invested in myself that I have had the opportunity to model for numerous businesses as well as have my photos displayed on a national level.

My modeling opened even more doors for me. I began to network with people who accepted me for who I was. Thanks to those who saw the potential in me, I was able to grow as a woman, model and entrepreneur. As I matured, I wanted to share a similar network of opportunities with others. I saw myself nurturing other women's talents so that they too could realize their full potential. I wanted to be more than a model; I wanted to be an inspiration and role model.

***

About eight years ago, I came out of a major depressive episode related to health and work stress. I lost my faith, and not even a mustard seed remained. You could see just by looking at me that I was in a dark place; I wore sweatpants with no makeup and my hair was unwashed. I wasn't the fashionable Charlie that you see now.

My sister often took me to the doctor or emergency room and my mother would pray for me, saying that God told her to "check on her baby." My best friend was also a great support. She spoke life into me and rubbed my back. She's the kind of person you want in your life!

I am so grateful for my team of doctors and my therapist. I completed some healing exercises and wrote affirmations on my bathroom mirror with red lipstick. I spoke the affirmations out loud until they became easier to say. In that same restroom, I had several breakdowns, where I would literally find myself crying in a ball on the floor or slumped over the edge of the tub, having to force myself to speak the affirmations.

I began to work on myself like never before. I listened to inspirational, motivational and transformational speakers. In order to be more valuable to those around me, I had to learn how to rescue myself first. I invested in personal and professional development, including entrepreneur classes, and I finally started my blog.

Forgiveness was the ultimate catalyst to my healing. I absolutely had to forgive myself. First of all, for the bad choices I made and second, for continuing to give others power over my life. And in order to truly heal myself and become free, I had to forgive anyone who ever hurt me along my life journey. Sometimes people say hurtful things and don't realize the mental pain they inflict. I remember replaying the memories over and over in my head for years. I'd think to myself, *why forgive when they were the ones who hurt me?* Damn! Forgiveness was a challenging one.

Trusting my gut was the ultimate act of finally trusting myself. I had a strong desire to fulfill my dreams and I finally believed that I could do so without the opinions of others. My gut told me that it was time to fulfill my dreams, and I knew without a doubt that there was no need to overthink it or ask anyone else's opinion on it. When you know, you just know! If it weren't for me trusting that feeling in my gut that made me feel so uncomfortable, I may not have had the opportunity to share my story.

Have you ever had a piercing gut feeling? It could have been related to anything such as your business, health, relationship, career, family, finances or friends. I imagine most of you have felt that intuitive gut feeling and can relate. Listening to your intuition allows us to take risks, leaps of faith and avoid unwanted situations.

***

The woman I see in the mirror today has been hurt. I will never forget the words I heard growing up. They're built into my memory and are a part of who I am. But so is the love I feel from those who believe in me. It is a choice to view things with a negative lens, and I choose to see the positive by reminding myself of how much I have, how short-sighted I was and how the moment I set my sight on more, doors began to open.

I've only shared a small glimpse of my life. But I do not wince as I share that pain. Rather, I embrace vulnerability, because I know that is where my strength lies. Through years of addressing self-confidence and mental concerns, I have welcomed the help of therapists and medical professionals. It takes a village to become this powerful.

My story is still writing itself. I know that my story may frighten some and inspire others. I know that I am not alone and that there are others like me who hide their scars due to the fear of being judged or defined by their experiences. I have devoted myself to uplifting women because I know what self-confidence can do. I understand how lack of self-esteem can derail your life simply because you feel as if you are undeserving.

As adults, my mother and I have begun to mend our relationship. Since my childhood, I've seen the sun, I've seen joy and I've experienced happiness. I sought help and I became better. I made the decision to no longer allow the negative words to define me. And now, I pass the pen to you so that you too can share your story and hopefully help someone who needs it.

My name is Charleszetta Baldwin, and I am a survivor of child abuse.

***

More than 2.9 million child abuse cases are reported annually[1]. Just imagine those cases which are not reported. Imagine those who do not get to share their story or cry out for help. Although abuse is common, it is not normal. If you are a survivor of child abuse, know that it is not your fault and that you are powerful. No matter what your abuser says or how many people overlook your red eyes, bruised emotions and pain, you are worthy of happiness. You are worthy of acceptance. You are loved.

If you wish to seek peace, please reach out for help. There are alternatives. You do not have to live through this pain just to be happy. Call 1-800-344-6000 for assistance. Your educators, coaches and mentors are all mandated child abuse reporters. They will help you.

Signs of emotional abuse: rejection or withdrawal of love; verbal put downs; perfectionism; negative prediction (e.g. 'you'll never amount to anything'); negative comparison (e.g. 'Why can't you be more like sister?'); scapegoating; shaming; cursing or swearing; threats; and guilt trips (e.g. 'How could you do that?')

Let's Reflect Workbook Activity

1. How long has it been since you truly loved yourself?

   _____

2. When did you decide to put yourself first in order to begin your healing process?

   _____

3. Will you acknowledge your trauma so that you can begin your transformation process?

   _____

4. When will you forgive yourself?

   _____

About Charlie

Charlie, known as "Charlie on the Spot" to her social media supporters is quickly making her mark on the Bay Area fashion, art, and music scene.

Since deciding to take a leap of faith and build her own brand five years ago, the model, host, and fashion blogger influencer has been strutting down her own runway of success. Charlie's natural ability to connect with the camera, as well as with key target audiences has landed her numerous gigs with major national and local brands and influencers such as: Sulmers, Angel Brinks, Diishan Imira "The Black Hair King of Silicon Valley for Mayvenn Hair," pro football player and BeastMode Founder Marshawn Lynch, and Mika McCant, Owner of Spoiled Boutique, to name a few.

Down-to-earth and all about her business, Charlie serves more than just "face." With a background in fashion design and merchandising, as well as a bachelor's degree from California State University East Bay, she also utilizes her talents behind the scenes as a Creative Director who styled dozens of photoshoots and cast music videos for major recording artists including Dice Soho's "SSP," featuring Ty Dolla Sign & Desiigner.

Fashionable and free-spirited, Charlie has a natural ability to uplift and inspire everyone she comes into contact with. She uses her growing social media platform to empower and inspire women from all walks of life to embrace their own unique brand of beauty.

In addition to her fashion blog and social media tribe, Charlie, a Bay Area native, mentors young girls, who like her, have struggled with overcoming learning disabilities and self-worth issues to continue beating the odds.

Credits:

Makeup Artist: Ahlaya Reed Artistry

Contact Information:

Website: Charlieonthespot.com

Email: charlie@charlieonthespot.com

Instagram: @charlie_onthespot

Facebook: Charlie on the Spot

Chapter 5

Trauma to Transformation
Butterfly Principle: It's Not Your Fault

WALKING OUT OF HELL INTO HEAVEN

By: Tamela Gospel

Being molested as a child

It began when I was five and continued for many years. I remember it was a cold rainy night in November the first time it happened. I remember my mom leaving for work and telling me to take a bath and clean my room before she returned home.

While taking a bath, my mom's male friend invited me to his room for a minute, saying that he wanted to check me and make sure I had cleaned myself right.

After my bath, I went to his room as I was told and he directed me to the bed, where I was told to lay down. I felt confused and wondered what was going on. From that very first moment, my young instincts told me that something wasn't right. "Everything is gonna be okay," he told me, and I asked him, "What are you doing?"

"I'm just checking you to make sure you all cleaned up right," he said.

He lowered his head to my privates and began to touch me everywhere. I laid there, frozen, wishing that my mother was home. When he was finished, he told me to go put on my pajamas and prepare for bed. I walked into my room and put my pajamas on as I was told. Even though I was only five, something inside told me that what he did wasn't right. So, I knelt down to the floor and asked God to cover me. I thought of my mom, who I always heard say, "Lord, cover my children."

Later that night, he came into my room and said to me "It's our little secret, don't tell anyone." "Okay," I replied.

"That's my big girl," he said, handing me a piece of candy as he left. I set the candy down on my dresser and sat on the floor of my bedroom while I waited for my mom to return.

When she finally came home, my mom came into my room to check on me.

"Are you okay?" she asked.

"Yes, but can I sleep with you?"

"Sure, I'll come in your room and we can sleep together."

I was so happy because I didn't want to be alone. I didn't tell her what happened, because I didn't know at the time that it was the right thing to do. I just wanted to be with her. I believe my mother knew something wasn't right though, because she kept asking me if I was sure that I was okay. And I kept reassuring her that I was fine.

He continued to molest me for many years. And then other people did. My uncle. A friend of the family. Cousins. I didn't know how to tell anyone what was going on. Thus, I kept it all to myself. As I grew older, I became angry, mad, and frustrated, wondering why older male figures continued to take advantage of me. I felt as if I were everyone's target, as if they were all trying to hit the $100 bullseye. I remember that despite one of my uncles being married, he molested me. I'll never forget the night when I was about thirteen or fourteen, and it somehow got out to all of my friends and family that he had molested me. I felt so embarrassed and afraid. Anytime someone would see me, they'd ask, *Is it true? Did this happen to you?* and *Why did it happen?*

With all of the questioning, I began to hate life. I began to feel unworthy, unclean. My boyfriend at the time also found out. What an embarrassing moment! Although I had wanted to share it with him, I just couldn't. I felt that I'd be judged, unwanted and mistreated if I had opened up about what had happened to me. It finally got to the point where I felt that enough was enough.

So, one day, the man who started it all was upset with me because I hadn't done one of my chores. He began to yell at me, but I knew the real reason why he was mad. He was upset because he wanted to touch me again and I told him no. By that time, I was in my early teens and I knew that what he had been doing was wrong. I had had enough!

I went straight to my mother and told her that this wasn't about the chores. It was because I wouldn't let him touch me. I finally spoke the truth to my mother, "How about him being mad because I won't let him molest me anymore? How about me being mad because it seems as if I got molested by everyone? I feel like everyone's throw 'round puppy!"

Once my mother knew what had happened and for how long it had been going on, the police were called, and he was removed from the house. My mother then apologized to me and said she will do her very best to make sure it wouldn't happen to me ever again. I know she felt bad, but I felt worse. I knew how hard she worked to make ends meet and make sure we had what we needed in life.

When it came to the molestation, some of the perpetrators got far and some didn't. But how far they got with me didn't really matter, because touching someone—especially an innocent child who is taught to trust adult figures in their lives—in any way that they do not want to be touched is wrong. And it should never happen.

Growing up, I tried to move past what had happened. One incident after the other. But it seemed as if every time I tried to build myself up, another man would molest me, tearing me down once again. I grew up feeling unsure about life and with so many mixed emotions. I wondered, "Why me?" and "When will this ever stop?"

Feeling unsure, heartbroken, and incomplete, I began to look for love in all of the wrong places. At fifteen years old, I ended up pregnant. I did not have a job and I was still in school. Knowing that I would soon have a baby to care for, I tried to put myself in a position to graduate on time. Luckily, I was able to do so, but I struggled. Prior to being pregnant, I had struggled in life. It just felt so hard for me. Becoming a mother did not make the struggle any easier. In order to graduate on time, I had to go to night school and summer school on top of breastfeeding and caring for my young baby. My emotions and feelings were all over the place, especially because I had always told myself that I wouldn't have a baby until I was married, which didn't happen.

Since the very beginning, my daughter's father has been, and still is, consistently involved and supportive. When I found out I was pregnant, I wasn't in the best place mentally, physically or emotionally to be the very best mother that I could be. And I felt that having a baby with all of those feelings wasn't a good thing. But her father always reassured me that we would be okay.

The journey of discovering my pregnancy

I was in the shower and I remember noticing that my breasts were huge! They seemed to have grown overnight! Not thinking much of it, I continued with my shower. When I was through, I was approached by my mother. "Wow, so when were you going to tell me about your pregnancy? You're only a baby."

"No time soon, because I'm not pregnant," I told her.

"You might not know right now but you are pregnant. I can see it all in your face." Knowing that being pregnant was a possibility, I thought to myself that I ought to get checked out. I knew that my mother had access to my records at Kaiser, so I scheduled an appointment at Planned Parenthood, where my mother would not be able to find out.

The appointment was scheduled about a week after my mom voicing her suspicion of my pregnancy. I went into the appointment feeling incredibly scared and nervous. My stomach was tied into knots. Nothing my mother said was ever wrong or incorrect; it was like she knew everything even though she'd tell me, "I don't know everything." She could have fooled me!

They called my name and directed me to the back to take my vitals. My heart rate was elevated because I was so afraid. "Is everything okay?" the nurse asked. "Yes," I said with my mouth, although my heart was jumping and screaming, "No!"

"Well, I'm asking you," the nurse said, "because your heart rate has increased along with your blood pressure."

"I'm sorry," I told her, "I'm only fifteen and I'm here, as you know, to get a pregnancy test and I'm extremely scared, nervous, and I feel like a disappointment for even being here in this position. I always said I wasn't having kids 'til I married, which was my heart's desire and here I am sitting in your office." All types of thoughts began to flood through my head: *What if everyone is upset? What will I say to my mom? What will I do about school? Who should I tell first if I am pregnant?* The nurse looked at me reassuringly, "I need you to calm down first so that your vitals can come down. Don't freak out over something that we don't have the results to yet. Let's do one thing at a time young lady."

I began to calm down and I prayed, telling God, "If this is what you want for me, then I will have this baby because you give life. But Lord, I'm so afraid, please hold my hand and forgive me for my sins of having sex before marriage, I've truly learned my lesson. Father God, please walk with me through this journey if this test is positive...and if I am pregnant, then I'm really about to learn." Once my vitals were stable, I was placed in a room where I waited for what seemed like forever. By the time the nurse practitioner walked through the door, I was just about ready to pass out on the floor.

"Hello, how are you?" she asked me.

"Nervous and afraid," I told her.

"You are going to be just fine, I've seen situations like this before."

"I'm praying that I will be."

"Well," the nurse practitioner said, "your test results are positive, you are three months and four days pregnant."

A wave of disappointment washed over me, and I began to cry my eyeballs out. I didn't want to be a disappointment to my mother nor to God because I had been raised in a church and had always wanted to be pleasing in God's sight. In my eyes, what I had done wasn't good. But as soon as I got home to my mother, she looked me in my eyes and said, "God got you more than anybody can have you and He is the only one who can give life and take it away, so you'll be just fine, hold your head up and just walk it out."

Next, she asked me what I was going to do about school, and I told her that I would continue. "I'm gonna graduate on time and I'm gonna walk the stage with my daughter in my arms."

I did everything I could to follow through with the promise I made to my mom. I went to night school, I stayed up late, I took extra tests, I did extra work and whatever else I had to in order to make sure I graduated with my class. And at the end of my senior year, I did exactly that, with my daughter there to witness.

While becoming a teenage parent, I lost some friends and some loved ones. Many people told me that I would never grow up to be anything. Many told me that I should kill my baby, get rid of it, that I would never make it with a baby and that all I'd ever be was a dropout. The negativity went on and on.

The words and opinions of others were painful and didn't feel good, but I knew I couldn't just throw in the towel. Friends who I thought would never leave my side talked about me, saying how stupid I was to get myself into that position without really knowing the trauma that I had dealt with prior to becoming pregnant.

I had finally found a male figure who loved me unconditionally and who didn't take advantage of me. Why couldn't I just peacefully live my life and be happy with him? Feeling sorry for myself, I began to do the "why me" cry.

On top of seeking love in the wrong places, I had been drinking and partying frequently, trying to cover up the pain I still felt from my childhood trauma. The pain that I was still dealing with on the inside. I was a mother, and I knew that I couldn't carry on the way I had before; I now had a baby girl looking up to me. My spirit became bothered.

The overcoming part I will never forget

It was a very cold night. I was in my twenties and pregnant with my second daughter. It seemed that every day, God was putting on my mind that I should change my ways and return to him. I avoided his voice until years later, after having my second daughter. I heard the Lord telling me, "Come back to me, my child, I'm waiting for you." He repeated himself, over and over, for about a month straight. I had been going through so much during that time, and I continued to hear the Lord telling me to come back to him. So on that cold night, I sat on the edge of my bed and I finally responded. "Lord I hear you and I'm coming back to you. I'm done. I can't live this life the way I am right now."

I didn't have a car. But the next Sunday morning, I borrowed a car and was driving on my way to a church that I had never been to before. I only knew the name of the church along with the verbal directions that my coworker had given me. I prayed the whole drive there that I'd find the church I had been invited to.

Through only the power of the Holy Spirit as my guide, God led me straight there. I was guided to that church, not by navigation, but by the Holy Spirit, and I am so grateful that the Lord is real and that I was able to make it to the church on that day.

I walked into Living Waters Deliverance Ministry, hoping to see my friend there—and there she was! I walked up to her and gave her the tightest hug, thanking her for inviting me.

From the moment I set foot in the church, it felt as if the weight of an elephant fell off of me; that's the only way I can think to describe the feeling. On that day, I gave my life to Christ and from that very moment, my life changed from the inside out. It seemed like everything had changed and all for the better. I'm glad that the Lord called me and that I heard him.

There is a scripture that I have always hung onto, a scripture that has taken me through everything previously and has always spoken to my spirit, giving me the strength to not give up.

> *Be strong and courageous. Do not be afraid or terrified because of them, for the Lord your God goes with you; He will never leave you nor forsake you.*
>
> *– Deuteronomy 31:6*

Rather than remain a victim of my past, I have chosen to pick up the stones thrown at me and build myself upon them into a changed, renewed, set free, and unmovable woman of God. I encourage those who read my story and can relate, or those who have gone through their own turmoil, to always hang onto God's unchanging hand. For if it weren't for him, I would not be the woman that I am today. I would not be able to tell my story because I would still be allowing my past to control me.

As long as I am living, I will continue to stand alongside every woman and child who has been molested or pregnant during their teenage life. I want you all to know, first of all, that it is not your fault, and second, that your life is not over; it is only beginning. I encourage you all to rise above, with an open heart, unto God so that He can transform you as well, from the inside out into whatever He has called you to be in this life. Build your story, find your voice and share your testimony with the world as I have done. You too can write your story and walk into your truth.

Let's Reflect Workbook Activity

1. What are some things in your life you are blaming yourself for?

   _____

2. Who in your life do you need to forgive? Do you believe that forgiveness is for you and not your abuser? Why or why not?

   _____

3. What in your life would you change in order to heal your traumas you have dealt with or are dealing with? Do you have regrets? Why or why not?

   _____

4. What does self-love look like for you?

   _____

5. *Psalms 139:14 I praise you because I am fearfully and wonderfully made; your works are wonderful, I know that full well.*

Psalms 34:8 Taste and see that the LORD is good; blessed is the one who takes refuge in him.

I had to put this scripture to work and try his word and through his word I receive my true healing and change within because God is the true healer of all things.

What does this scripture mean for you?

About Tamela

Nurse Tamela Gospel is a Christian Life Coach, Motivational Speaker, Self-Love Coach, and Co-Author. "The woman who serves unnoticed and un-thanked is a woman who loves God more than she desires the praise of others," Tamela states.

Tamela helps change lives in adults and children who had the patience, knowledge, and wisdom to deal with whatever came. Tamela is a believer of God and always receives with the help and covering of the Lord Jesus Christ.

Contact Information:

IG: @michellegospel

Email: tea.gospel30@gmail.com

Non-Profit: Women of Worth (W.O.W.)

Website: www.beautyforashes.org

Facebook: www.facebook.com/tamela.michellegospel.com

Part 3: Believe Me

Chapter 6

Butterfly Principle Trauma to Transformation: Your Past Does Not Define Who You Are!

Kill the noise of your past, free the little girl inside, don't silence your hurtful places, live your life the way you want to!

Don't Silence Her

By: Shardae Jones

My name is Shardae Jones. I am a Mother, Entrepreneur, Student, and Author here to share my story of how I went from being a runaway teen who made devastating choices to a strong, unapologetically bold woman. I learned to love myself unconditionally through prayer, a positive mindset, breaking down barriers with a bomb therapist, and filling up my space with motivated women.

Your mind is the most powerful thing in the world. If you can change the way you think, you can change the way you feel, and I guarantee you can change your life. We can't operate without the brain working at its full capacity. The most important thing to remember is we are children of God. Children meaning, we are forever growing, changing and evolving in him daily so we will always make mistakes. It's all in the bounce back.

My story will allow you to read about some of the challenges, heartaches of growing pains, and sins that the Lord himself has forgiven me for. Yet, his undying love and forgiveness still puzzles me today. I recall looking in the mirror at myself and seeing a woman who was not quite up to par. My goal is to share my story in order to free myself and to help heal another woman in the process. I aim to motivate and inspire all women to know that their past does not define them. I want you to understand the only validation you will ever need is from God.

Motherless Girl

I want to explain my backstory on how I grew up and some challenges I have faced as a young girl. I did not have the best relationship with my mother growing up. I felt angry with her for living her life without me being a part of it, and I felt a huge sense of abandonment. She missed all of my first moments: my first boyfriend, my first period, my first heartbreak, and the birth of my first-born child. My father was there for it all and raised us by himself for a long time. I can remember growing up and giving my dad Mother's Day and Father's Day cards at one point. I have one of the best dads on the planet. However, I still found myself longing for my mom.

I have to acknowledge the woman who came into my life at such an important moment. I was turning twelve and had started my first period. I used to call her "the car wash lady." That's where she met my father. We did not always see eye to eye. She taught me how to think differently, be respectful, and dress stylishly yet professionally. I did not know how to receive her love. I fought it but she won my heart and she is my mom. I learned how to develop and make my relationship with God real through her guidance. She is smart, educated, classy, and a simply phenomenal woman. The most important thing I admire is her relationship with God. She loves the Lord and practices the behaviors she teaches. My mom would show up at my school while I was trying to cut class and say, "The Holy Spirit told me to come down to this school." Mama bear has Jesus on speed dial! Thank you to all the women who are motherly figures, who love children regardless of biological connection.

Throughout the years I would try and ask her a million questions about her life like, "What happened mom?" She never quite gave me her story and I desperately wanted to know her side. I wanted my son to know his mother was young and imperfect but, that she was also not afraid to be her true authentic self. I won't silence myself and neither should you! Join my movement #dontsilencehermovement.

Don't Silence Her is the beginning of a movement to allow women to share their stories in a safe space to heal themselves and others. This gift of writing I have, I received from her. Mom, your story may have been silenced but your legacy will live on. My mom passed away from a heart attack in August of 2016, at only fifty-nine years young. The death of my mother put me in a bad head space. I was not taking care of myself and feeling very depressed. Every day I am still missing my mom. I reached out and was blessed to find a Christian-based therapist who worked with me. At first, I would just go and lay all my problems on her table and every week she would say did you do your homework? What are you doing to make a change for the better? Every time she would let me know I needed to do the work. One day I decided just maybe she was right, and I began my journey to transform.

Operation Transformation

Here we go. It's time to transform my life. This should be easy. All I have to do is journal, read, meditate, pray and go conquer the world, right? Let me say nope, it's deep and you have to dig through raw, uncut emotions and years of pain and trauma. Past pains of untold stories that linger within us. Just remember even untold stories can cause some of the drama we lived out in our childhood that eventually played out into adult life. I walked into my therapist's office thinking I was only there to deal with my issues around my mom, but I discovered so much more.

The biggest shame and traumas I had to work out in therapy were abortion, low self-esteem, rape, the death of my biological mother and a million other things. The pain from my trauma is heavy. My mind felt as if it was fighting off spiritual gangrene that would not be healed. No drugs were being used to numb my pain. It was all my mental health playing tricks on my every thought. I was pregnant at the age of sixteen by a boy who I thought loved and cared for me. When I became pregnant, his exact words where "You better kill that little motherf***, man."

Those words cut like a knife in my heart. We argued every single day and night. This was a form of the abandonment trigger of my mother. He doesn't want me or the baby. No one cares about me. How did I let this happen? I felt so alone carrying my baby. I was so tired of fighting with everyone. I decided this was all too overwhelming for me and I couldn't go through with having a child. I terminated my pregnancy. The after pains were damaging for my mind, body and soul. I cried for months straight. *I sank into a deep depression.* I felt extremely ashamed of myself. I felt worthless. I felt raging anger inside. I felt extremely unattractive. Every day was a dark day for years of my life. I would cry when I saw another teenager pregnant and having her baby. I felt inadequate for not having the strength to keep my child.

Below is an insert from a journal I kept while going to therapy. This helped free me inside:

"Lord knows my heart and how I wanted each child who graced my womb, I am not proud of terminating my pregnancy, but it must be a part of my purpose. This pain may never go away but at least I know I faced it head on, I have written and spoken my truth and I have to forgive myself. Forgive the girl who lacked the courage, who was too afraid to do it alone, who was scared, lost, and seeking validation in all the wrong places."

Changing Mindset

I want to leave my readers with tools that can be used to begin a transformation. The first step is to pay attention to your feelings. There is nothing wrong with seeking a therapist to aid in taking care of your mental health. I found my therapist through Psychology Today online. Second, find a healthy hobby to help take your mind off stressors in your life. Practice self-love. There is power in a woman's voice and her story. Respect the woman who has had to endure unimaginable pain. Don't silence your past emotions, experiences, or traumas, for these are what make you the beautiful woman you are today.

Affirmations

If you do not have anyone to encourage you, begin the process of loving and affirming your damn self. Start with some things that are simple yet powerful. Create a vision board of goals and future aspirations. Dream freely again. Read self-help books! Burn sage and say affirmations daily: *I am enough, I can do anything I set my mind to, I am a child of God, I am a powerhouse woman, I am destined for greatness.*

You are a gift and inside your gift box is something unique and spectacular. I am not what happened to me, I am what I choose to become.

Let's Reflect Workbook Activity

1. How will you serve and honor yourself each day?

   _____

2. How will you begin your process of self-love and daily affirmations?

   _____

3. Will you let go of your trauma and step into your transformation?

   _____

Dedication

This is dedicated to my biological mother and any woman who has felt the need to silence her story. I will leave you with a quote by her:

"You'll have dreams, thoughts and fears you will and think of things you don't understand, you will cry out in pain, and time will come to a standstill, and what will you do? Will you cry? Will you die? Will you try? Try to see to go on, try to take care of you."

- Francine Hall Jones.

Butterfly Principles:

Your past does not define who you are!

Kill the noise of your past, free the little girl inside, don't silence your hurtful places, live your life the way you want to!

Don't forget to dream, work towards, and imagine the best version of you every single day.

About Shardae

Shardae Jones is an entrepreneur, Co-Author of Butterfly Project, Mother, Student and most importantly child of God. Shardae has a YouTube channel with positive thoughts and motivational real talks. Overall, Shardae is just a work in progress and every day she makes strides to be a better woman!

Credits:

Hairstylist: Joshua Bone/ Salon Philosophie

Makeup Artist: Shardae Jones

Lashes: @idripluxuarylashco

Shardae@dontsilencerherperiod.com

Contact:

Website: www.dontsilenceherperiod.com

Instagram: @Jbugmom

Part 4: Witness Me

Chapter 7

Trauma to Transformation
Butterfly Principle:

Give yourself permission to heal, not get over it, but get through your experience.

Permission to Heal

By: Tracey Frison

M y eyes start to peer open slightly, blinking as I am awaking from what feels like a deep state of unconsciousness or sleep. I hear muffled conversations nearby. My body feels weak and tired, some parts are even numb, so I try not to move. Instead I continue to look around, scanning the room for clues as I try to piece together what had just taken place. As I'm still regaining consciousness, I hear a baby crying in the distance.

At twenty-one years old I had just graduated from college, moved into my first apartment, and started a new job. Things were finally falling into place for me. I enjoyed my new routine of working during the week and spending time with my family and friends on the weekend. I had a somewhat rough childhood dealing with being raised in poverty and homelessness, so these accomplishments were a big deal to me. I was finally feeling a sense of normalcy.

By the time I was twenty-two years old, I found out I was pregnant. I was overwhelmed with mixed emotions. I felt happy, yet nervous, not knowing what pregnancy or motherhood would bring. I finally started to feel a sense of completeness. In the early months into my pregnancy I started to experience what seemed to be morning sickness, but I noticed that as time went on, I became more ill. My morning sickness would last past the morning well into the evening, and wouldn't subside for days at a time. This left me feeling miserable. I was unable to work, eat, or sleep much due to me spending so much time in and out of the ER. That's when I started to notice something wasn't right.

A doctor had finally diagnosed me with hyper-emesis, a condition of 24-hour bouts of uncontrollable vomiting in most cases during pregnancy. Before I was discharged from the hospital, I was sent to ultrasound receiving further explanation into why I was so sick. I was pregnant with identical twins. I could barely wrap my head around having one baby, let alone two!

For the next few months I was watched very closely by my prenatal network. I took very good care of myself and followed all of the doctor's orders, however I still constantly remained ill. Every little pitter patter of movement and hearing their little hearts beat at my routine doctor's appointments brought me pure joy. I was in love with them already. One evening I decided to try to unwind and relax by taking a bubble bath. I had been feeling anxious all day and was having a really unsettling gut feeling. The bath didn't calm me much. I grew more anxious and decided to go to the ER. Because of how far along I was in the pregnancy, I was able to go straight to the Labor & Delivery department that time. I was placed in a room where a nurse assisted in placing me on a baby monitor. Heart and fetal sounds were being picked up on the monitor. This was reassuring for me, but the medical staff was still concerned so they sent me to get an ultrasound right away.

During the ultrasound exam I began to doze off. It was the middle of the night and this particular time the exam was unusually long. As I noticed the technician was just about done with my exam, I could sense the change in his demeanor as the room became strangely eerie and quiet. He turned to me and said, "I found the heartbeat for Twin B but there isn't a heartbeat for Twin A. That baby has passed." In that very moment I felt my heart shatter into a million pieces and words couldn't describe how I felt. I immediately started crying.

At that point, the doctors from my prenatal network were aware of the situation so I was admitted into the hospital to await further instructions. Shortly after, one of the doctors came into my room to talk to me about the action plan going forward. The first doctor tried to send me home to make funeral arrangements for both babies stating, "Whatever happened to Twin A will soon happen to Twin B so you should experience that in the comfort of your own home." I couldn't give up that easily. I immediately asked for a second opinion. The second doctor explained to me that they were going to need to deliver the surviving twin. However, at 25-weeks gestation the chances of my baby surviving were around 20% so I would need to continue to carry both babies as long as I could.

A few days later I was encouraged to attend a therapy group while in the hospital for grieving mothers. This left me with very conflicting emotions as I was mourning the loss of a child that I was still carrying as well as trying to mentally and emotionally prepare for the birth of my living baby. The next morning, my baby's heart rate and oxygen levels started to drop. I was rushed to the operating room for the doctors to perform an emergency cesarean. That morning my surviving son was born at 26-weeks gestation weighing only 1 pound, 2 ounces. I couldn't hold him or feed him because he was so fragile. He was placed on a ventilator and incubated shortly after birth. Later that day, the nurse brought me my deceased son swaddled in a blanket and matching hat. I was able to spend a few final moments with him before he was taken away to be cremated.

A week later I was discharged from the hospital but not the same way all the other moms were discharged. They were wheeled out with their babies. I was wheeled out with a memory box of my deceased child. I really started to feel the pain both physically and emotionally. I left home pregnant and returned home with nothing. Over time I shut the world out, isolating my thoughts and feelings, and never sharing with anyone how I truly felt. I was in a really dark place. It was difficult trying to mourn the loss of my deceased son yet at the same time trying to stay strong and hold myself together for my son fighting for his life in the NICU.

My faith was really being tested. I was angry, hurt, and my heart full of resentment asking God why me as I cried myself to sleep every night. I felt less of a woman and that I failed as a mother not being able to properly birth my child into this world. All of these thoughts and emotions left me feeling broken. Even though my son's life was short lived, the love I had for him felt like an eternity. All my life

I had been told all you need is the faith of a mustard seed. Well, at that point, I felt like that was all I had. Every day I held on to that mustard seed as I went to the hospital to care for my baby.

After a few months he was finally well enough to go home. Going to the hospital was different this time. This was a highly anticipated moment for me, a moment that I could only imagine. As I said my final goodbyes to the hospital staff one of the nurses approached me and said we have to give you a proper send off. So, she had me sit in a wheelchair as she handed me my baby swaddled in a blanket. Overwhelmed with emotion, tears of joy streamed down my face. I finally was able to have my moment with my baby like all the other moms. A year later, I gave birth to a beautiful healthy baby girl.

As time went by, I still hadn't grieved. The devastation was far too great, so I took all of that pain and buried it inside of me. For years I carried the weight of depression, sadness, anger, and resentment. In a dream I was startled by a noise just outside of my room. As I peered out into the hallway my deceased son was wandering throughout the house. I would call out to him, but he wouldn't respond; he just continued from room to room. When I woke up, I was in shock and disbelief. That was my first time dreaming about my son. I knew it was a sign and he had a message. What I interpreted from my dream was that his soul was still wondering this earth. I needed to let go of all the painful emotions I held inside so he could cross over. It was almost as if he came to give me permission to heal. I felt like he was saying "Mommy, it's okay." That weekend I scattered his ashes in the ocean, freeing him as well as myself from all of the pain I had become a prisoner of.

Let's Reflect Workbook Activity

1. Have you ever had a loss? If so, how have things been since your loss?

   _____

2. What are some emotions Tracey shared in her story that you can relate to?

   _____

3. Have you given yourself permission to heal? If not, then how can you?

   _____

4. What are some healing tools you practice or would like to practice?

   _____

About Tracey

"When life gives you lemons, make pink lemonade"

-Tracey Frison

Tracey Frison is a Registered Respiratory Therapist, Corporate Executive Administrator, Co-Author, and Mother of three.

Tracey would love to work with displaced/homeless women with children. Tracey has a passion to help women get back out into the world and workforce. She helps women by empowering, encouraging, and hosting uplifting workshops and events for women and young girls who are the most vulnerable. Tracey is looking forward to being a guest speaker/advocate and sharing her story and experiences of growing up homeless.

Contact/Booking:

email: traceyfrison@yahoo.com
traceyfrison52@gmail.com
IG: @trayonce_711
Facebook: Tracey Frison

Resources:

Grief Share Hotline: 800-395-5755 (US and Canada) or 919-562-2112 (International)

Suicide Prevention Hotline: 1-800-827-7571

Teen Hope Line: 1-800-394-HOPE

****

Trauma to Transformation Butterfly Principles:

How to use these principles and apply them towards your healing process. Use these tools for your healing toolbox.

1. Stop Being a Victim
Candyce Pirtle-Smalls, LVN

No one owes you a damn thing, take responsibility on your part. Stop thinking and acting like a victim. Self-care and self-love will allow you the power to set yourself free. Give yourself permission to heal, free your mind, body and soul.

2. The Act of Giving and Receiving
Teisha Levi, LMFT

Forgive myself for everything, including my participation.

3. Self-Value
Ericka Parker

The regard that something is held to deserve; the importance, worth, or usefulness of something. A sense of one's own value as a human being: feeling of self-worth or self-esteem.

4. Forgiveness
Charleszetta Baldwin "Charlie on the spot"

Forgiving myself and others was a key element along my transformational journey.

5. It's Not Your Fault
Tamela Gospel

Being molested is not your fault; being a teen mom is not your fault.

6. Your Past Does Not Define Who You Are!
Shardae Jones

Kill the noise of your past, free the little girl inside, don't silence your hurtful places, live your life the way you want to!

7. Permission to Heal

Tracey Frison

Give yourself permission to heal, not get over it, but get through your experience.

Conclusion

N ow that you have read and completed all of these powerful stories from these brave and courageous women, you see you are not alone. Feel free to reach out and connect with these women to share how they have touched you, inspired you or resonated with you. We invite you to join our movement. We are on Facebook and Instagram @fit_butterfly_innovation.

About the organization:

F.I.T. Butterfly Innovation Inc. (Female Inspired Transformation) is a Non-Profit organization in Walnut Creek, California serving East Bay and Bay Area.

F.I.T. is a safe space for teens, women of domestic violence, sexual assault, trauma, grief, teenage pregnancy, or codependency. It is a place for women who want to be heard or seen, witnessed, and believed in so that they can experience recovery and healing.

We collaborate and partner with individuals and

organizations offering free services such as inner healing workshops.

Please write to us or visit our website for a list of services and to learn how you can donate or get involved.

Website: www.fitbutterfly.org

Email: info@fitbutterfly.org

Address:

1990 N California Blvd Suite 20

Walnut Creek, Ca 94596

**We accept all donations

About the Author

Candyce Pirtle-Smalls is a nurse, educator, life coach and author of the new book, <u>Mindful Meal Prep: Clean, Delicious Recipes for Weight Loss.</u> Known as "Coach Candy," she is passionate about helping women become the best version of themselves—mind, body and spirit. Candy successfully transformed herself from the inside out when she shed 50 pounds off her petite frame with clean-eating, weekly meal prep and exercise. Today, Candy uses her experience to coach others along their transformation journey via her 90-day, one-on-one coaching program.

Founder and CEO of Fit in Her Kitchen Meal Prep Candy's Kitchen, LLC, Candy is a Certified Holistic Health Coach and Behavior Change Specialist. Candy serves on the Walnut Creek Chamber of Commerce, has facilitated a 30-week weight-management class on behalf of Kaiser Permanente Medical Center and served as a nursing professor at Unitek College. Candy works with teens in a mental health treatment center as a Facility Manager.

Committed to turning her life's pain into passion, Candy is a Certified Advocate for domestic violence awareness and prevention. She volunteers for other nonprofit organizations, such as "Girl Talk" which helps build self-esteem in tween/teen girls and she sponsors workshops for young men within the juvenile justice system.

Whether it's in the kitchen, virtually, by phone, or in one of her weight management classes, Candy inspires, educates and motivates individuals to lasting change. Candy is the mother of one adult son and lives with her husband in the San Francisco, Bay Area of California.

"No Woman Left Behind"

IF YOU'RE MAKING A DIFFERENCE AND A POSITIVE IMPACT TO OTHERS IT DOESN'T MATTER WHAT THE FORECAST OF CHAOS MAY LOOK LIKE AROUND YOU

@ANTTONIODESIGNS

Made in the USA
Middletown, DE
23 December 2020